MEET OUR FLAG, OLD GLORY

by **April Jones Prince**   Illustrated by **Joan Paley**

LITTLE, BROWN AND COMPANY
New York ↝ Boston

Meet our flag, Old Glory.
She's red and blue and white.

Her stripes are like a peppermint's;

Her stars are big and bright.

Old Glory is America —
She belongs to me and you.

She waves above this wondrous land
Singing, "Make your dreams come true!"

I show her that I'm faithful
Before my school day starts;
I pledge allegiance to the flag
With my hand upon my heart.

Whenever I spy Old Glory
I feel so strong and proud.

I see her at the ballgame
Soaring high above the crowd.

I place her near lost loved ones.

I wave her to a tune.

She flies outside my own front door.

She's even on the moon!

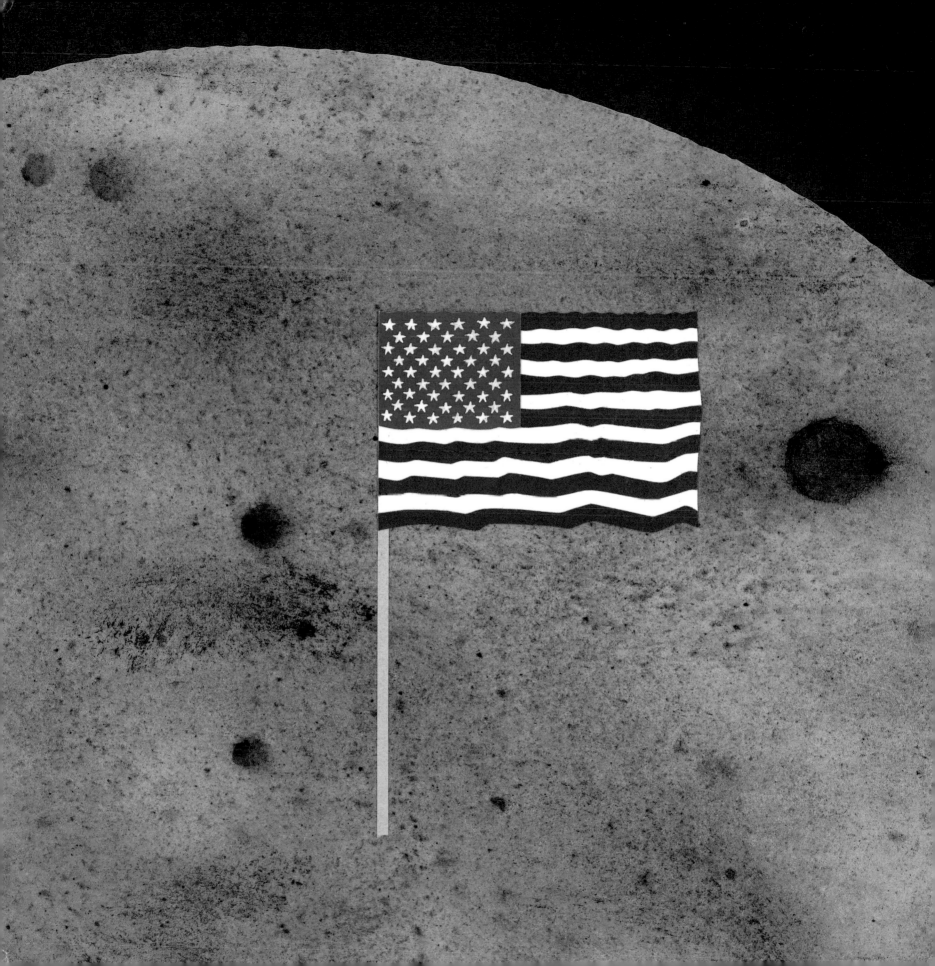

She stands for all our heroes —
Courageous, strong, and brave.
She reminds us of the freedoms
They've fought to win and save.

Old Glory's all around us,
A bold and brilliant sight,
Especially on the Fourth of July . . .

When her spirit lights the night.

Old Glory's Story:
A Brief History of the American Flag

Old Glory is the oldest and most important symbol of our country, the United States of America. But our flag did not always look the way she does today. Where did she come from, and what does she mean?

Beginnings in Britain

The United States began as thirteen colonies ruled by Great Britain, an island 3,000 miles away. The British flag (often called the Union Jack) flew over the colonies in America for more than 150 years.

Union Jack, flown in America 1607–1775
The British flag combined the English cross of St. George (red) with the Scottish cross of St. Andrew (white).

In 1775, the colonists decided they did not want to fly the Union Jack any longer. The colonies had come together to protest what they felt were unfair British laws and taxes. To show their unity, American colonists created the Grand Union flag. It had thirteen stripes to represent the thirteen colonies, and a small Union Jack to show that the colonies were still loyal to Britain.

Colonial leaders in Congress tried to settle their disagreements with Britain peacefully. But the British king, George III, and his government would not listen to the colonists' requests. The colonies decided to break away from Britain. On July 4, 1776, Congress adopted the Declaration of Independence, which proclaimed the colonies to be "free and independent states." The United States of America was born.

Grand Union flag, 1775–1776
This flag was also called the Continental Colors or Congress flag.

"A New Constellation"

The new country needed a new flag. But first there were war plans to make and carry out; Britain was not going to let its colonies go without a fight. It was June 14, 1777, when the new flag was born. On that day, Congress passed a resolution stating: "Resolved, That the Flag of the United States be 13 stripes alternate red and white, that the Union be 13 stars white in a blue field representing a new constellation."

The "Stars and Stripes" had one star and one stripe for each state. The stripes matched those on the Grand Union flag. But stars were a feature new to national flags; most national flags at that time showed royal or religious symbols. The American flag's "new constellation," or new group of stars in the sky, was symbolic of the new nation — a kind of nation ruled not by kings and queens but by and for the people. Americans would choose their own leaders and make their own laws. They would strive to live up to an ideal stated in the Declaration of Independence: that all men are born with an equal right to live, to be free, and to pursue happiness.

The resolution of 1777 did not explain the meaning of the flag's colors. But a resolution passed a few years later described the colors' use in another national symbol, the Seal of the United States. Red stands for courage, white for purity and innocence, and blue for loyalty and fairness.

The flag resolution also did not specify how many points the stars were supposed to have, or how the stars were to be arranged. Some flagmakers placed the stars in a circle. Others put them in rows, in the shape of a larger star, or scattered randomly against their blue background.

Legend has it that Philadelphia seamstress Betsy Ross sewed and helped design the first flag, telling General George Washington that she could cut five-pointed stars much easier — with one snip of her scissors! — than the six-pointed stars Washington had proposed. Betsy Ross did sew American flags, but we do not know if she made or designed the first one. The Stars and Stripes may have been created by a committee. Most historians think that Francis Hopkinson, a signer of the Declaration of Independence from New Jersey, was one man who played a significant role in our flag's design.

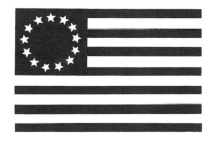

"Betsy Ross" flag, 1777

Placing the stars in a circle was meant to show that no state was better than any other.

A "Star-Spangled Banner"

The first change to our flag came in 1795, after two new states had joined the Union. Two stars and two stripes were added to the flag. This fifteen-star, fifteen-stripe banner flew during the War of 1812, which the United States fought against Great Britain. An especially large flag soared above Baltimore's Fort McHenry. During a battle there in 1814, the flag inspired a young American lawyer named Francis Scott Key to write a poem about the "star-spangled banner." The poem was set to music. The "Star-Spangled Banner" became our national *anthem,* or official song, in 1931. It is one of the world's few national anthems devoted to a flag.

The United States continued to grow. By 1817, five more states wanted to be represented on the flag. Congress decided to add only stars from now on. The flag went back to having thirteen stripes to honor the thirteen colonies that fought for independence. This allowed each new state to be represented without changing the look of the flag

too much. Congress declared that a new star would be added to the flag on the Fourth of July after a state was admitted to the Union. Since 1777, the flag has changed twenty-six times. Our current, fifty-star flag has flown since 1960, the year after Hawaii became the fiftieth state.

"Star-Spangled Banner," 1814

The flag at Fort McHenry measured 30 feet by 42 feet. It was sewn by Mary Pickersgill of Baltimore, along with her mother, two nieces, and her 13-year-old daughter. You can see the flag today at the Smithsonian Institution in Washington, D.C.

There was once a question whether to remove stars from the flag. From 1860 to 1861, eleven states from the South left the Union and formed the Confederate States of America. During the four years of civil war that followed, some Americans thought that eleven stars should be taken off the U.S. flag. But President Abraham Lincoln insisted that the stars of those states that had left the Union remain on the flag. In 1865, the Civil War ended, and the nation was reunited under the Stars and Stripes, or "Old Glory." This nickname for our flag, originated by a Massachusetts sea captain named William Driver in 1831, became popular during the Civil War.

Confederate Battle flag, 1861–1865

The thirteen stars on this Confederate flag represented the eleven states that joined the Confederacy, and two states that Confederates had hoped would join, but never did.

Pledging Allegiance

On October 12, 1892, the 400th anniversary of Christopher Columbus's landing in the Americas, 12 million American schoolchildren pledged allegiance to the flag for the first time. A man named Francis Bellamy, who worked for a popular children's magazine called the *Youth's Companion,* wrote the Pledge to give American children a special way to honor their flag. Today, students in many American schools say the Pledge every day, although no one can be forced to say it.

The words of the Pledge have changed a bit since 1892. Today they are:

I pledge allegiance to the flag of the United States of America, and to the republic, for which it stands, one nation under God, indivisible, with liberty and justice for all.

What do these words mean? A *pledge* is a promise; *allegiance* is loyalty. So pledging allegiance to the flag means promising to be loyal to your flag and your country, *the United States of America.* Our country is a *republic,* which means we choose leaders to make our laws. The nation is *indivisible,* meaning it can't be broken apart. And in our nation, we try to give every American the same freedoms and fair treatment — *liberty and justice for all.*

When you pledge allegiance to the flag, stand tall, look at the flag, and place your right hand over your heart. If you're wearing a hat, it's polite to remove it and hold it over your heart.

Spying Old Glory

Do you know why Old Glory flies outside most churches, schools, and sports arenas, and above government buildings such as courthouses and voting places? She flies to remind us of the liberties we enjoy every day. We are free to worship as we choose. We can learn, travel, work, play, and live where we are able. We are free to speak our minds, as long as what we say does not take away the rights of others. We have the right— and the responsibility— to elect our lawmakers and to shape our own futures.

Old Glory flies outside homes and stores as well, when we want to display *patriotism,* or loyalty to and love of country. This is especially true on national holidays such as Presidents' Day, the Fourth of July, and Flag Day — Old Glory's own holiday. On Memorial Day, we place flags at cemeteries and war memorials to honor the many Americans who have died protecting our country and our freedoms.

In 1969, American astronauts Neil Armstrong and Edwin "Buzz" Aldrin became the first humans to set foot on the moon. They raised Old Glory as a sign of peace and achievement.

Old Glory is usually, but not always, a symbol of patriotism. During most wars of the past century, Americans across the country have flown Old Glory to show support for U.S. soldiers. But during the Vietnam War, in the 1960s and 1970s, Old Glory was often used as a symbol of protest. Many Americans were against the war in Vietnam. Some expressed their anger by cutting, burning, or writing or trampling on Old Glory. In 1989, the Flag Protection Act made these demonstrations illegal. The Act was overturned by the U. S. Supreme Court in 1990, however, because these actions are a form of free speech — a right protected by the First Amendment to the U.S. Constitution, the supreme law of our land.

The United States is not perfect, but it is a nation that tries to live up to what Old Glory represents: liberty, opportunity, hope, and justice for all. People have come from all over the world to become Americans. That makes us diverse in race, religion, background, and ability. Old Glory helps bring us together. She stands for our past and our present — from thirteen colonies to fifty states — and for our future. She stands for me and you.

A Flag for Waving, and for Celebrating

The National Flag Code, established in 1923 and modified several times since, gives guidelines for displaying Old Glory. There are no penalties for not following the Code. The most important thing to remember is that Old Glory is considered a living symbol of America and should always be treated with respect.

★ Old Glory should never be allowed to touch the ground or floor.

★ Old Glory should fly at night only if the flag is properly lit.

★ Old Glory should not fly outside in bad weather, unless the flag is weatherproof.

★ Old Glory should always be raised quickly and lowered slowly, as if you are eager to see her flying but reluctant to take her down.

★ If a flag is faded or beat-up, it should be retired in a dignified manner, preferably by burning.

★ No flag should fly higher than Old Glory on American soil. (The only exception is at United Nations headquarters in New York City, where the United Nations flag flies higher than the flags of all the member nations.) When Old Glory flies with other flags, she should be placed either at the observer's left, or at the center and highest among the flags.

★ Flags are flown at half-staff when a government official or other important person dies. Displaying the flag in this way is a sign of mourning. When flying Old Glory at half-staff, you should first raise her to the top of the flagpole and then lower her to half-staff. She should be raised to the top of the pole again for an instant before being lowered.

★ When a person in the military or in government service dies, a flag is draped over his or her casket. The stars go over the top left of the casket, where the person's heart would be. Before burial, the flag is removed, folded, and given to the person's family.

★ When Old Glory is folded correctly, her triangular shape resembles that of the tricornered hats worn by Americans fighting for independence from Britain during the Revolutionary War.

★ A flag raised upside down is a sign of distress that should be used only in times of great emergency.

For more information about Old Glory and the U.S. Flag Code,
contact the National Flag Foundation at 1-800-615-1776
or visit www.americanflags.org

Also illustrated by Joan Paley:
Little White Duck
One More River

For the everyday heroes who hold our flag high and inspire America's children to become informed, engaged citizens; for Mom, Dad, and Chip, who taught me the value of integrity and hard work; and for David, whose passion for words rekindled my own.
—April Jones Prince

To all our courageous men and women who stand to protect and preserve our freedom. And to President George W. Bush for pledging to be faithful to our flag and the freedom for which it stands. And especially to Bianca, my sweet, precious, and ever-present friend.
—Joan Paley

The author would like to thank David White at the National Flag Foundation
for his thoughtful review of the factual portion of the text.

Little, Brown and Company • Time Warner Book Group
1271 Avenue of the Americas, New York, NY 10020
Visit our Web site at www.lb-kids.com

First Edition

Library of Congress Cataloging-in-Publication Data

Prince, April.
   Meet our flag, Old Glory / by April Prince ; illustrated by Joan Paley. — 1st ed.
      p. cm.
   Summary: Rhyming text introduces the American flag and some of the patriotic events with which it is associated. Also includes the text of the "Pledge of Allegiance."
   ISBN 0-316-73809-3
   1. Flags—United States—Juvenile literature. [1. Flags—United States.] I. Paley, Joan, ill. II. Title.

CR113.P75 2004
929.9'2'0973—dc21   2002041636

10 9 8 7 6 5 4 3 2 1

PHX

Printed in the U.S.A.

The collage illustrations in this book are made up of shapes cut from different papers, which are painted with watercolor and textured with crayon, pastel, colored pencils, and oil paints. The layered shapes create a three-dimensional effect. The text was set in Gadget and Rockwell, and the display type was handlettered by the illustrator.